rosie O'DONNELL

America's Favorite Grown-Up Kid

Tanya Lee Stone

A Gateway Biography

The Millbrook Press
Brookfield, Connecticut

For Leah Harris, My Funny Girl

Cover photograph courtesy of Globe Photos

Photographs courtesy of Corbis Sygma: pp. 1 (Robert Visser), 28, 40 (Robert Visser);
Globe Photos, Inc.: pp. 4 (© 1999 Lisa Rose), 6 (© 1997 Judie Burstein), 16 (NBC), 20
(© 1998 Albert Ferreira), 22, 23 (© Judie Burstein), 25 (© 1995 Milan Ryda), 35 (© Judie
Burstein), 37 (© 1999 Andrea Renault), 39 (© 1997 Laura Cavanaugh), 42 (© 1997 Judie
Burstein); Everett Collection: pp. 9, 17, 19, 31; Photofest: pp. 11, 21, 24, 27; © Neal
Preston/Corbis: p. 32; © Yvonne Hemsey/Liaison Agency: p. 38

Library of Congress Cataloging-in-Publication Data
Stone, Tanya Lee.
Rosie O' Donnell: America's favorite grown-up kid / Tanya Stone.
p. cm. — (A Gateway biography)
Includes bibliographical references and index.

Summary: A biography of the comedian, talk show personality, and awards show host.
ISBN 0-7613-1724-4 (lib. bdg.) ISBN 0-7613-1338-9 (pbk.)
1. O'Donnell, Rosie—Juvenile literature. 2. Comedians—United
States—Biography—Juvenile literature. 3. Motion picture actors and actresses—United
States—Biography—Juvenile literature. 4. Television personalities—United
States—Biography—Juvenile literature. [1. O'Donnell, Rosie. 2. Comedians. 3.
Entertainers. 4. Women—Biography.] I. Title. II. Series.
PN2287.027 S76   2000
792.7'028~092—dc21
[B] 99-462282

Published by The Millbrook Press, Inc.
2 Old New Milford Road
Brookfield, CT   06804
www.millbrookpress.com

Rosie O'Donnell

Rosie readies herself for the 12th Annual Nickelodeon Kids' Choice Awards.

4

It is May 1, 1999. Eight thousand screaming, cheering fans are packed into Pauley Pavilion in Los Angeles, California. The teen band 3rd Storee is singing and dancing. Endless confetti rains down on everyone's head. "And now, here's Rosie!" shout the announcers.

Rosie O'Donnell bursts on stage, arms waving, yelling "Yeah!, Yeah!, Yeah!" at the top of her lungs. She's dressed in orange sneakers and a bright blue shirt. She picks up a big plastic ball at her feet and kicks it back into the audience. "Are you ready to have fun?" she hollers, and the crowd goes wild.

The hottest stars of Hollywood have gathered for one of the most popular award shows of the year. Is it the Grammys? The Emmys? The Tonys? No, it's the 12th Annual Nickelodeon Kids' Choice Awards. Rosie is hosting the show for the third time in a row. This award show is special because kids from all over the country choose the winners. For the 1999 awards, more than six million kids cast their votes. After the event Rosie told reporters, "I like this show the best. It's the easiest and most fun to do. I always feel like I'm just being invited to a big party."

Lately, it seems that much of Rosie's life *is* one big party. She has become a movie star and is thought of as America's sweetheart by many. And her talk show success has been huge. But life was not always so easy for this funny, outgoing girl from Long Island.

On March 21, 1962, Edward and Roseann O'Donnell had a baby girl they named Roseann. (She didn't get the nickname Rosie until years later.) She was the third child, but the first girl. Her older brothers are Edward Jr. and Daniel. Over the next few years, Roseann's parents had two more children—Maureen and Timothy.

The five O'Donnell children grew up in a house in Commack, New York. Their grandmother also lived with them. Roseann shared a bedroom with her sister, with

whom she is still very close. The family was not poor, but they did not have a lot of money either. They had a station wagon with an AM radio and did not shop at fancy department stores.

The O'Donnells lived in a neighborhood filled with kids where the tomboyish Roseann could play all kinds of outdoor games. She loved kickball, softball, skateboarding, and basketball. When she was eight, her older brothers' Little League coach let her practice with the boys. She later remembered, "I was always the first girl picked for the neighborhood teams." Rosie also liked to paint and write in her diary.

One of the kids who lived in her neighborhood was Jackie Ellard. She lived across the street. Jackie and Rosie became best friends. (As an adult, Jackie has helped Rosie with some of the jobs that come with fame, such as sorting through tons of her friend's fan mail.)

Rosie's favorite hobby as a kid was paint-by-number pictures.

From the time she was little, Rosie loved to sing and make people laugh. Even by the age of four, she knew she wanted to perform for people. In first grade, she told jokes at show-and-tell. And in second grade she played Glinda the Good Witch in *The Wizard of Oz*, practiced signing her autograph, and sang "Second-Hand Rose" for the talent show.

It was her mom's idea to sing that song because they both loved Barbra Streisand. The older Roseann was a big fan and sang Streisand songs around the house all the time. That same year, she took her young daughter to see Streisand's new musical movie *Funny Girl*.

Rosie's mother had a lot to do with who she is today. Her mom loved music, theater, and the movies. She was light-hearted and funny, always quick to make people laugh.

Rosie says, "One night I was watching my mother at a PTA meeting making everyone laugh. I was about five, and I remember thinking, Wow, that's a good thing." Rosie's mom also had a talent for making the holidays special. Halloween and Christmas were exciting at the O'Donnell house. But while Roseann was still just a young girl, something happened that changed her life forever.

When Rosie was ten, her mother became very sick. She and her brothers and sister visited her when she had to go to the hospital. But within just a few months, on March 17, 1973, Roseann Murtha O'Donnell died. She was only thirty-eight years old. It would be many years—in fact, when Rosie was thirty-four years old herself—before the O'Donnell children learned that their mother had died from breast cancer.

Losing a parent at any age is hard. But when you are still a kid, it can shatter your whole world. The O'Donnell children were suddenly without a mom. And making things worse, their father, Edward O'Donnell Sr., was too sad and distant to help his children understand what was going on. He did not even allow them to go to their mother's funeral. Left without a mother and—in many ways—without a father, Rosie and her sister and brothers had to learn to take care of themselves.

Rosie ended up taking on a lot of the household chores, looking after the other kids, and taking care of her grandmother. It was a huge burden for a little girl. Luckily, she got a lot of love and support from Jackie Ellard's mom, Bernice. "I was raised at the Ellards' house. I ate dinner there four nights a week."

Rosie once won a pogo-stick contest by bouncing to the beat of Elton John's "Crocodile Rock."

Television had always played a big part in the lives of the O'Donnell family. And it got even more important after Roseann O'Donnell died. The young Roseann was especially attracted to shows that had single-parent families or mother figures that showed up to take care of a family. Shows such as *Nanny and the Professor*, *My Three Sons*, and *The Partridge Family*, as well as the movies *Mary Poppins* and *The Sound of Music*, were comforting to her. But sadly, "There was no Julie Andrews [the nanny from *The Sound of Music*] coming in. We sort of took care of ourselves and raised each other." As an adult Rosie says, "Television took the place of parenting." In addition to these family shows,

Julie Andrews playing guitar in a scene from a movie Rosie loved as a child, **The Sound of Music**

11

Rosie also spent a lot of time watching the variety talk shows *The Merv Griffin Show* and *The Mike Douglas Show*.

Although parts of her life were hard, Rosie remained kind and funny. In junior high, she met a teacher named Pat Maravel. Mrs. Maravel, Rosie's math teacher, cared about Rosie and paid special attention to her. Rosie said, "She helped me stay focused and feel loved, and I think she had the biggest effect on me. She took me under her wing." Rosie says that Maravel was also the first adult to say I love you to her. "Those were three words simply not uttered in my house." (To this day, Bernice Ellard and Pat Maravel get Mother's Day cards from Rosie.)

In high school, Rosie baby-sat for all the neighborhood kids, played shortstop on her softball team, and was class president her senior year. And this was in addition to her many duties at home. She loved sports and later said she was "a regular tomboy jock girl and proud of it." Rosie was even crowned Homecoming Queen and Prom Queen.

Anyone could tell that Rosie was meant to entertain people. She was always in school plays and loved to perform for people. Her bedroom was plastered with pictures of stars such as Barbra Streisand and Bette Midler. (When Rosie later met Barbra Streisand on her talk show, she said with tears in her eyes, "In many ways to me it feels like my mom walking through the curtain. You were a constant source of light in an often dark childhood.") And she had scrapbooks filled with ticket stubs and other reminders of events she saw.

Rosie O'Donnell knew from a young age exactly what she wanted to do. Partly because her father wasn't paying enough attention to make his kids stick to the rules, Rosie went to New York City to see movies, concerts, and theater every chance she got. To Rosie, becoming a movie star seemed out of reach, but theater was a different story. Waiting outside a stage door after a play or musical she thought, "On this block, in this theater, people are doing what I hope to do."

In high school, Rosie was elected Class Clown and Most School Spirited.

At the end of her senior year, Rosie performed at the Senior Follies. There happened to be a comedy club owner in the audience. After the show, he invited Rosie to perform at his club. She soon saw a new comedian perform on television—Jerry Seinfeld. When she got up on stage at the comedy club, she used the jokes she had heard and the audience went wild! Afterward, she found out that the man who had hired her was very angry. Comics are not allowed to use each other's jokes—they have to write their own. Rosie decided to get some experience by just introducing other comics. After that, she was ready to try again. But comedy is harder than it looks. She says, "I was 17 when I started …When people didn't laugh, I thought *they* were stupid.…I had that 'try anything' attitude. But I had to *learn* how to be funny onstage."

But Rosie had her heart set on being an actress, not a comic. She left Commack to go to college. She spent a year at Dickinson College in Pennsylvania, but didn't do well. Then she went to Boston University to study theater. Halfway through the year, a professor told her she would never become an actress. With that, the strong-willed Rosie left college behind.

She decided that she would get the training she needed to make it as an actress by polishing her comedy act. She performed in comedy clubs all over the East. "I always did [comedy] with the hopes that someone would see it and put me in a sitcom, a movie, or a Broadway show," says Rosie. It took a few years, but she got her first break on a talent show called *Star Search* shown on national television. Rosie was the first female comic ever to win first place.

Rosie quickly learned that one "break" did not mean that your career would take off. She still spent the next few years working as a comic—and it wasn't always easy to find work. But Rosie did not give up. Her next important break came one night while doing stand-up in a Los Angeles comedy club. A man from NBC television saw her act and decided to give her a role in a show called *Gimme a Break*. Rosie was finally going to be a character on a TV show! She played Maggie O'Brien for the show's final season.

After that, she got a job at the television music channel VH-1 as an announcer. She was so funny and did so well that she was given her own show called *Stand-Up Spotlight*. The show featured comics and Rosie was the host. Using her brains as well as her talent, Rosie made sure she was involved in the business end of the show, too. That way, she helped choose the comics and shared in the profits. Before she was finished, Rosie was nominated for two awards for *Stand-Up Spotlight*. Now she was really on her way.

A publicity photograph from NBC for the show **Gimme a Break**, in which Rosie played the main character's funny neighbor.

Rosie was no longer an unknown person trying to find work in show business. Based on her success, she got a small part in her first movie—*Car 54, Where Are You?* Two years later, she was hired for another television show. This one was called *Stand By Your Man.* Although good experience for Rosie, neither the movie nor the TV show was successful. But Rosie's star was about to shoot through the sky.

In 1992, Rosie got what really was her big break. Director Penny Marshall hired her for *A League of Their Own*. In fact, she thought Rosie was so funny that she changed part of the story to fit Rosie better. Rosie was excited just to be meeting Marshall, who used to star as Laverne on one of Rosie's favorite shows as a kid—*Laverne and Shirley*. (Rosie and Penny Marshall would later make some funny TV commercials for K-Mart together.)

Rosie was cast as Doris Murphy in *A League of Their Own*. She was great in this movie that reminds us that women can do anything, including cheering up America during World War II by playing professional baseball with every ounce of heart and soul that men do. Actresses were not hired for that movie unless they could play baseball well. "I was the only one who could throw the ball from third to first, so I got the job," Rosie remembers humbly.

Rosie also met singing star Madonna on that movie. Rosie has always been star-struck and she was very nervous about meeting Madonna. But the two women had one powerful thing in common—they had both lost their mothers at a young age. They felt close to each other right away. In the movie, they played best friends. And although they are very

Rosie is on deck in **A League of Their Own**, which also starred Tom Hanks, seen behind Rosie, and Madonna.

19

different kinds of people, they became best friends in real life. "Madonna is some exotic food, and I'm just a peanut butter and jelly sandwich," says Rosie.

That same year, Rosie could hardly believe it when she was given the chance to present an award at the 44th annual Emmy Awards! She also appeared at charity benefits. Her next movie was *Sleepless in Seattle*, where she met actress Meg Ryan and director Nora Ephron. Rosie was quickly getting known for being one of the nicest, funniest actresses to work with and she made fast friends with both women. Ephron said of Rosie, "When you meet her, you want her to be your friend."

Rosie was on a roll. Next up, she got a part in the movie *Another Stakeout* with Richard Dreyfuss and Emilio Estevez and was on the television show *Living Single*. And in 1993 she was chosen to be Betty Rubble in the movie *The Flintstones.* One of the things that came out of that movie made her incredibly happy—kids all

Rosie's favorite video games are Pac-Man, Tetris, Asteroids, and The Legend of Zelda.

A scene from the 1993 movie **Sleepless in Seattle**, also starring Meg Ryan.

Rosie as Betty Rubble, in **The Flintstones**

over America voted her their favorite movie actress. About her first Nickelodeon Kids' Choice Award, Rosie beamed, "When a kid says you're all right, that means you're doing something right in your life." The other was that her image as Betty Rubble became a Flintstones McDonald's Happy Meal doll. "The doll actually looks like me, and she's sort of chubby which is kinda cute." Rosie also got to meet one of her favorite stars on that movie set— Elizabeth Taylor, who played Betty Rubble's mother.

Even with all of the wonderful things happening to her, Rosie had yet to reach her longtime goal of performing on Broadway. But during a break in filming *The Flintstones*, she got herself an audition for the part of Rizzo in *Grease!* (It wasn't easy because she is not really a singer or a dancer.) The day of the audition she happened to be on the show *Good Morning America*. Rosie grabbed that chance to make herself better known to the *Grease!* people and burst into a song from a musical on national television!

She not only got the part, she worked hard, sang pretty well, and was very funny. She got both good and bad reviews, but many who saw her thought she was terrific. And at the end of the show on opening night in New York, Rosie came out and said to the audience, "This is such a wonderful night; it's a dream come true. The only sad part is that my mother didn't see it."

During that time, she was asked to present at the Academy Awards. She and her sister and mother had always had fun Academy Award parties when Rosie was a kid and she was thrilled to be at the real thing. "Look at me, I'm on the Academy Awards! Can you believe it?" she told the audience. She also got to give out an award at the Tony Awards show, which honors Broadway.

Rosie was now a star in demand. After *Grease!*, she made several more movies, including *A Very Brady Sequel* and *Now and Then*. *Now and Then* was about four childhood friends who get together when they are older and remember the times they shared. Rosie loved to spend time with the actresses who played the young friends (Gaby Hoffmann, Christina Ricci, Thora Birch, and Ashleigh Ashton Moore), telling a reporter, "We hang. We play Twister." Rosie also did stand-up comedy again, performing in big clubs and doing a special called *HBO Comedy Hour*. But once again, Rosie's life was about to change.

The cast of **Now and Then**, a movie Rosie enjoyed making and which got good reviews.

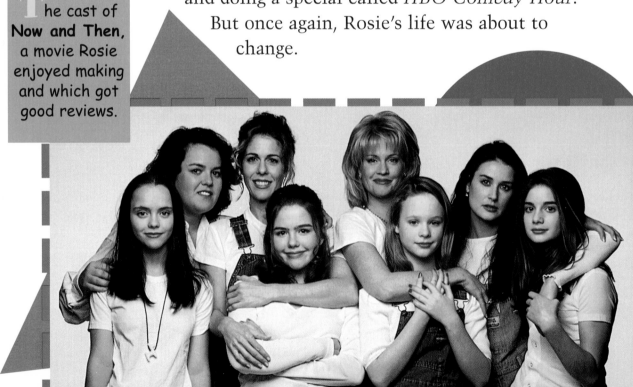

Even when she was a kid herself, Rosie always loved children—baby-sitting neighborhood kids and looking after her brothers and sisters. As an adult, she wanted a child of her own more than anything and said, "I always knew I would have children. It was never a question." In May 1995, Rosie adopted a baby boy. She named him Parker Jaren O'Donnell. Rosie tries hard to make sure that her fame doesn't put the spotlight on him, "*He* didn't choose a career in showbiz, *I* did."

A few months later, Rosie took Parker with her to film the movie *Harriet the Spy*. It was based on a book that she had loved as a kid. Rosie played Ole Golly and became good friends with eleven-year-old Michelle Trachtenberg, who starred as Harriet. In fact, Rosie liked to

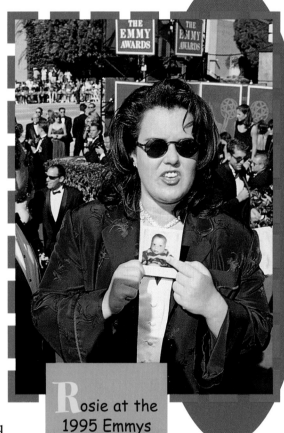

Rosie at the 1995 Emmys holds up a picture of her newly adopted son Parker.

spend a lot of time playing with the young actors and actresses. She gave airplane rides, thumb wrestled, and even made up a cherry-spitting game.

She had a blast making that movie and also made time to be in a movie called *Wide Awake*. But Rosie decided that a busy schedule that took her away from home was not what she wanted for her new family. She was ready for something that would let Parker "sleep in his own bed every night."

That something was Rosie's talk show. She wanted to create a daytime show like the ones she used to see as a kid. Rosie told *Time* magazine that she "tried to make a show that an eight-year-old kid could watch with his mother and grandma that would entertain everyone." And she succeeded. *The Rosie O'Donnell Show* began in June 1996 and was an instant hit. *Newsweek* called her "The Queen of Nice." *Newsday* said, "Rosie is like a twelve-year-old kid opening Christmas presents."

The great thing about Rosie's show is that she is just as excited as her viewers are about meeting the guests. She is a huge fan of everything show business. The president of the

Audience members on "The Rosie O'Donnell Show" always find a carton of milk and a Drake's snack cake on their chairs.

A scene from the well-loved **Harriet the Spy** movie, in which Rosie played the wise and wonderful Ole Golly.

It's 1996 and Rosie has her own television show!

company that produces the show said, "She's been preparing for this show all her life. Whether it was singing Broadway tunes with her mother or memorizing...*The Partridge Family*."

Rosie truly admires and respects the people she invites on her show. Unlike many shows on daytime TV, she won't bring up a subject that her guest doesn't want to talk about. You don't have to watch *The Rosie O'Donnell Show* for very long to see that she is having the time of her life. On one show, just before bringing on a star she adored, Rosie turned to her bandleader John McDaniel and said, "I love this job."

Rosie knows the words to so many songs she has been called a "human juke-box."

Rosie does have one of the best jobs in the world. She gets to meet anyone she thinks is talented and great. Rosie likes to invite all different kinds of entertainers to her show. She brings on stars from the movies, television, and Broadway. She often invites entire casts from Broadway shows to perform. This way, people all over the country—instead of just in New York—get a taste of a Broadway show. Sometimes Rosie performs too. When she had the cast of *Bring in Da Noise, Bring in Da Funk* on, she wowed the audience with her own talents as a drummer. (Rosie played drums in a rock band while in high school.)

Since Rosie's show began she has flung about 20,000 Koosh balls from her desk!

Rosie also has ordinary people on the show who have done great things. It could be a person who helped someone else, or a terrific teacher, or even a fireman who has saved the day. And, of course, there are the kid guests. Rosie loves to have kids on her show and has interviewed both child stars and regular kids who have done cool things. Some of her famous kid guests have been Mary Kate and Ashley Olsen, Ryder Strong, Anna Paquin, and Madylin Sweeten. Rosie has also shown the talents of thirteen-year-old singer Charlotte Church and done spin art with ten-year-old painter Alexandria Nechita.

In February 1998, Rosie invited five-year-old geography whiz Christopher Montoya on her show. And in September of that same year, she asked the entire Little League World Series Championship team to join her. She gave them tons of presents, including special baseball jackets, bats, and balls, and a promise to pay for a new batting cage that the Toms River, New Jersey, team needed. "She's a real cool lady. This was the best," said Gabe Gardner, one of the players.

In May 1999, while holding the show in Orlando, Florida, Rosie introduced the world to eight-year-old

Mallory Bacon. Mallory is a world champion barefoot water-skier and Rosie showed a video of the young athlete doing some tricks. In October 1999 she had eight-year-old opera singer Louis Lohraseb perform and gave him a trip to Italy with his parents. She also picks a few "Super Kids" from around the country and has them on her show. And don't forget Elmo from *Sesame Street*—he often drops by to say Hi and give Rosie a big hug!

Rosie with one of her special buddies, Elmo

Rosie with her ever-growing doll collection

Rosie's show keeps her very busy, but she still finds time for what is most important—her family. A little more than a year after *The Rosie O'Donnell Show* began, Rosie adopted a baby girl. She was born on September 20, 1997, and Rosie named her Chelsea Belle. Parker chose her middle name after Belle from the movie *Beauty and the Beast*. Rosie then adopted a third child. Blake Christopher O'Donnell was born on December 5, 1999. On her first show in 2000, Rosie told the audience her big news. "I have a new son. He's a beauty. I'm so happy."

There's no question that Rosie loves kids and that kids love Rosie. In 1997, Rosie hosted the Tony Awards and the kids of America voted her their favorite movie actress for the second time for *Harriet the Spy*. One reason kids adore Rosie may be that she is a big kid herself. Her host desk on the show is covered with toys. And she has one whole room in her house just for what her son Parker calls "Mama toys." "It's like a kid's playroom, except adult size. She has her collection of McDonald's Happy Meal toys on the shelves of her living room," said pal and actress Rita Wilson.

Rosie likes to sing "You Two" from the movie "Chitty Chitty Bang Bang" to her kids at night.

Rosie adores having fans who are kids and says, "I love kids, always have. It means so much to me to brighten up a kid's day." Kids can relate to many of the fun things she does on the show—it's almost as if she has invited everyone over to play. Once, she had actress Juliana Margulies eat her first-ever Twinkie for the whole world to see. Rosie is never afraid to look silly. When Super Kid Jaya Cox gave her Elvis glasses and sideburns, Rosie slapped them on and started to sing. And she and Jennifer Love Hewitt sang karaoke on her very own Rosioke machine!

Rosie also often picks audience members to come on stage and play games to win prizes. There are wacky trivia contests between her and her guests. She is forever shooting Koosh balls at a target in the theater! And Rosie always makes holidays fun, just like her mom did. For Halloween in 1998, she and her guests dressed up and "tricked" the audience. Rosie was Snow White, Billy Baldwin was Prince Charming, and Susan Lucci was the Evil Queen. And for Halloween in 1999, she taught everybody how to carve the perfect jack-o'lantern! She even made a holiday album and television special that year called *A Rosie Christmas*, with such stars as Elmo, 'N Sync, and Angelica Pickles from *Rugrats*.

Rosie O'Donnell is also a great role model. She thinks it is important for people—especially kids—to know that they should have oodles of self-confidence no matter what their body type is. Heavier than many show business females in the spotlight, she is happy with who she is and makes sure she sends that message out. She has said, "I don't want little kids who are overweight to think that looking like me is bad."
She is also concerned about kids who may be underweight. She adds, "Too many kids have eating disorders...I just want to be healthy." Focusing on being healthy–not too fat or too thin—makes Rosie an ideal role model.

Rosie's crush on Tom Cruise brought him to her show in December 1996, carrying an armful of roses.

34

When the Mattel toy company wanted to make a Rosie Barbie doll she told them, "If you'll make my Barbie with a real waist and a little double chin, I'll do it." And they did. Rosie even plays with her Barbie on her show, staging Rosie's Barbie's Theater like a true kid.

The Rosie O'Donnell Barbie doll

Rosie has done a lot to break the image that only thin is beautiful. She believes that being healthy—not weighing a certain amount—is the goal. She started a way for her viewers to get fit by creating the Chub Club. To her surprise, more than 300,000 people joined the club. The motto is "Eat less, move more," and people have done just that. "We're not talking about completely cutting out the Oreos. Just limiting yourself to four instead of eating the entire box," Rosie told members. *Health* magazine even gave Rosie a 1999 Fitness Crusader Award for her efforts to help people exercise and get fit.

Rosie has also learned that some people have reasons for eating too much. For her, she realized that it started when her mother died. A grownup Rosie later said that she linked "getting thin with getting sick and going away." In addition, she found the comfort she was missing in food. "Putting all that food inside me made me feel I was being filled up with love."

Most of all, Rosie understands that "people come in different sizes, shapes, and colors." When she co-hosted Nickelodeon's *The Body Trap* with Linda Ellerbee, it was clear to Rosie that kids need to be told that they are great people just the way they are. "I'm uncomfortable sometimes with my own body, but I'm never going to use it to [put down] myself, or to [put down] other women out there."

Rosie O'Donnell is also one of the most caring and generous people in show business. Even before she had her own talk show, she performed at many charity events. Rosie participates in too many to be able to talk about all of them. But some causes are particularly close to her heart—breast cancer and kid's charities.

Her mother's history with breast cancer has made Rosie aware of how important it is for all women to know about this kind of cancer. Each October she highlights National

Breast Cancer Awareness Month on her show. In 1998 she sent free T-shirts to women who got breast exams through her "I Got Squished" program. In 1999 part of each day's show had information about breast cancer. Some of this information was directed at kids.

Rosie is having a good time and doing good at the same time at the Arthur Ashe Kids Day in 1999.

On October 4, Rosie had model Christie Brinkley talk about a group called KIDS TALK: Kids Speak Out About Breast Cancer. And on October 8, Kids Konnected was featured. It is a support group for kids who have a parent with cancer and need a friend to talk to. An eleven-year-old boy named Jon Wagner-Holtz started the group in 1993. In addition, the Roseann O'Donnell Boutique was opened at a Manhattan hospital in honor of Rosie's mom. And in October 1999, Rosie published a book with her doctor, Deborah Axelrod. It is called *Bosom Buddies: Lessons and Laughter on Breast Health and Cancer*. All of the money that is made from selling this book will be given to breast-cancer charities.

Rosie cares so much about kids she says things like, "If there's anything I want to do with my celebrity, it's to make the world a safer place for kids." And, "I'm in a position to help children rise above any [problem], and that's the greatest gift you can give a kid." In February 1997, Rosie started the For All Kids Foundation. It raises money for groups working to help make life better for kids in need all over the country.

The money is raised in many different ways. Some of it has come from selling the Rosie Barbie doll and Tyco's The Rosie O'Doll—a cloth doll that talks. Money has also been raised by selling two books—*Kids Are Punny* and *Kids Are Punny 2*. The jokes, cartoons, and drawings came from real kids who had sent them in to Rosie. The foundation has already given away nearly $6 million.

In July 1999 actor Alec Baldwin said on

The Rosie O'Doll was created to raise funds for the For All Kids Foundation.

The Rosie O'Donnell Show, "There is no one in this [show] business, in the history of this business, who does more to help people than this woman right here … there is no one who even comes close."

In addition to her foundation, Rosie looks out for kids in other ways. In October 1999 she started a club called Rosie's Readers to encourage kids to read. Each week she picks a book. Kids at home read it and can e-mail what they think. She also does charity work for the Children's Defense Fund and gives advice to a program called Talking With Kids About Tough Issues. And at work, Rosie had a nursery and then a pre-school built so the staff's young kids could be near their parents.

All the earnings from Rosie's Kids Are Punny books go to the For All Kids Foundation.

Rosie is also very outspoken about gun control. On her show, she has pleaded for people to turn any guns they may have into the police. She has spoken out against the National Rifle Association (NRA), which is in favor of citizens having the right to own guns. And she believes that there should not be a single gun kept in any home where there are kids.

Rosie is not alone. Other celebrities are using their fame to get this important message heard. Actor and singer Mandy Patinkin helps to raise money and support for PAX, a group working to create an America free from gun violence. He said, "It is my hope and prayer that people like

Rosie O'Donnell will one day help us give my children and yours a world in which gun violence is a thing only to be found in history books."

Rosie's website has a link to Gun Free Kids, a site that educates people about keeping schools and communities safe from guns. And in December 1999, she decided to stop making commercials for K-Mart. The store is one of the main sellers of rifles in America and Rosie felt it was time to go their separate ways.

Rosie O'Donnell is a huge star and has won six Emmy awards for her work. She even manages to keep making movies. Hers was the voice of Terk in Disney's 1999 movie *Tarzan*. But even with her fame, the main thing that people adore about Rosie is how normal she is. "I think that's because everyone knows someone who's like me," Rosie says. She is a big star, but she still shops at Target and The Gap. "I'm just trying to be the same person I was in the beginning." And we love her for it.

About kids, Rosie has said, "Love them more than you think you should. There's no such thing as spoiling a kid. And keep loving them. That will give them security." *To* kids, Rosie says, "They should believe in themselves and believe in their dreams. If you believe it, you can live it. I know that to be true."

42

Rosie carries off an Emmy for her **Rosie O'Donnell Show**.

Important Dates

March 21, 1962   Roseann O'Donnell is born

March 17, 1973   Rosie's mother, Roseann, dies

June 22, 1980   Rosie graduates from high school

May 1995   Rosie adopts Parker Jaren O'Donnell

Rosie receives first Nickelodeon Kids' Choice Award for *The Flintstones*

June 10, 1996   *The Rosie O'Donnell Show* airs for the first time

February 1997   Rosie creates the For All Kids Foundation

April 1997   Rosie receives second Nickelodeon Kids' Choice Award for *Harriet the Spy*

May 22, 1997   Rosie receives Emmy Award for "Outstanding Talk Show Host"

September 1997 Rosie adopts Chelsea Belle O'Donnell

May 16, 1998   Rosie wins Emmy Award for "Outstanding Talk Show" and ties with Oprah Winfrey winning Emmy Award for "Outstanding Talk Show Host"

May 21, 1999   Rosie wins Emmy Awards for "Outstanding Talk Show Host" and "Outstanding Talk Show"

December 1999 Rosie adopts Blake Christopher O'Donnell

Sources Used

"Barbie Goes to Hollywood." *Parents*, September 1999.

Cahill, Gloria. "The Serious Side of Rosie O'Donnell." *Radiance*, Winter 1997.

Christian, Nichole M. "Another Day in Spotlight for Champions." *The New York Times*, September 3, 1998.

"Fitness Crusader Awards." *Health*, July/August, 1999.

Gerston, Jill. "Signoff; Making Happy Talk with Rosie O'Donnell." *The New York Times*. December 8, 1996.

Golden, Kristen. "Women of the Year: Rosie O'Donnell." *Ms.*, January/February, 1997.

Goodman, Gloria. *The Life and Humor of Rosie O'Donnell*. New York: William Morrow, 1988.

"Great Childcare: Women Who Make It Happen." *Redbook*, June 1998.

Kizis, Deanna. "Rosie O'Donnell: What She Really Wants—and It's Not Tom Cruise!" *Redbook*, November 1998.

Krohn, Katherine. *Rosie O'Donnell*. Minneapolis, MN: Lerner Publications, 1999.

Mair, George, and Ann Green. *Rosie O'Donnell: Her True Story*. New Jersey: Carol Publishing, 1997.

Michels, Victoria Kohn. "A Host Who's Silly, Passionate, Gushing and Glad." *The New York Times*, June 20, 1999.

"My Favorite Games." *Rolling Stone*, May 13, 1999.

Nash, Margo. "Rosie to the Rescue." *Intouch*: Cancer Prevention and Treatment: The Good Health Guide, October/November 1999, pp. 32–33.

Nickelodeon 12th Annual Kids' Choice Awards Video, Part I. Courtesy of Nickelodeon.

Parish, James Robert. *Rosie: Rosie O'Donnell's Biography*. New York: Carroll & Graf, 1997.

Powell, Joanna. "Rosie's Devotion." *Good Housekeeping*, June 1998.

_____. "Rosie's Worst Fear." *Good Housekeeping*, November 1999.

"Rosie by Rosie: What Makes Me the Woman I Am Today." *Marie Claire*, June 1999.

"Rosie O'Donnell: Cheerleader." *Time*, April 21, 1997.

Sanz, Cynthia. "Happy As They Are." *People*, September 29, 1997.

Scott, Janny. "Rosie Speaks, and Broadway Ticket Sellers Cheer." *The New York Times*, May 3, 1998.

"Sibling Revelry." *People*, December 1, 1997.

Smith, Liz. "Really Rosie." *Good Housekeeping*, June 1997.

Author interview with Mandy Patinkin.

Index

47

About the Author

Tanya Lee Stone is a former editor of children's books who now writes full-time. She is the author of several books, including *Diana: Princess of the People*, from The Millbrook Press.

In addition to her writing, Tanya runs Project Angel Food, an organization that she founded in 1997. Project Angel Food gathers food that would otherwise be thrown out by supermarkets and restaurants and delivers it to shelters and community centers.

She lives in Burlington, Vermont, with her husband, Alan, and her son, Jacob.